Sisterly Love Endures

Guidance for the Caregiver

By Jessie S. Myrick

Sisterly Love Endures: Guidance for the Caregiver

Publishing Services By: Pen Legacy®
Formatting By: U Can Mark My Word, Carla M. Dean
Cover Creation By: Kandieenterprises, Kimberly Martin
Edited By: Jackie Gardner

Library of Congress Cataloging – in-Publication Data has been applied for.

ISBN: 978-1-7362575-6-2

PRINTED IN THE UNITED STATES OF AMERICA.

All scripture references were taken from the New Living Translation (NLT) of the bible, unless noted otherwise.

Dedication

This book is dedicated in memory of Almete C. Simmons, my mother and first teacher. By her example, I learned how to care for others, and I thank God for the opportunity to care for her until her death. Also, to my other teachers, Willie M. Carter, my sister, Geneva Wells, my adopted "Granny," and all others who taught me how to give care and allowed me to provide care of any kind.

Table of Contents

Preface

According to **Love in Action**, a Bible study by Bill Hybels, when Christians receive salvation, God imparts three gifts: love, faith, and relationship. It is at that point that we begin to embrace who we are in Christ. These gifts alone enable us to do many things we would not naturally do, such as being called to care for a loved one at some point. Or we may even find ourselves in the care recipient position. When we receive these gifts with a sincere love for God, others, and ourselves, hopefully, fewer people will be left alone when they most need a warm touch and caring heart.

The gift of true and abiding love caused me to dig deep and uncover a part of me that I had not met. In providing personal care for my mother and sister, I discovered the ability not only to provide care for their simple, personal needs, but to my surprise, it also resulted in a total investment of the heart. In return, this investment rendered a payoff that I came to understand as unconditional love and sincere concern for others' wellbeing over my own. I managed to provide loving care to my sister while experiencing pain, feeling unappreciated, and many times being frustrated from my lack of understanding of her seemingly moody, mean-spirited attitude and refusal to cooperate with me. I learned when God is at work in the heart, then love, grace, mercy, and relationships can work together to shape life in amazing ways. The heart, mind, and soul then all work together with a spirit of humanity and community. Contrary to anything I may have wanted or thought necessary for myself was then neatly tucked away. I had to embrace the challenge of new learnings and attitudes required to care for my sister's every need. Over time, I was then able to acclimate to a different way of loving that became as natural as breathing.

The transformation I experienced caused me to think about many others who will find themselves experiencing life in a new and different world. Information from the National Alliance for Caregiving (NAC)[1] indicates that various forms of cancer, Alzheimer's, kidney disease, and pneumonia are increasing. Consequently, most people will inevitably experience either a life-changing medical event or know someone who has. Stroke, heart attack, cancer, serious accidents, mental disorders, or rare diseases can require lifestyle changes for all concerned. Whether you happen to be the care recipient or the person providing support, life will never be the same for a long time in many cases. During this time, both parties will require and appreciate encouragement, support, and a strong resolve to endure until the end.

My purpose in writing is to encourage you and assure you that what you are experiencing is truly part of God's grace for you. Stand firm in this grace.

1 Peter 5:12

[1]*National Alliance for Caregiving:*

To the Caregiver: A Note of Hope

Spiritual Reflection

Love is patient, love is kind. It does not envy, it does not boast, it is not proud. It does not dishonor others. It is not self-seeking, it is not easily angered, it keeps no record of wrongs. Love does not delight in evil but rejoices with the truth. It always protects, always trusts, always hopes, always perseveres. Love never fails.

1 Corinthians 13:4-8 (NIV)

What started out being my innate reaction to love and taking responsibility for my family's wellness concluded with a new perspective on life and keener insight on what happens when God moves the heart. It's about my divine assignment as my sister's caregiver; I like to refer to that time as our journey. This book is a memoir of my experiences as a caregiver, which, for me, turned out to be a life lesson in true love and spiritual enlightenment I shall never forget.

In my constant endeavor to grow stronger in my faith, somewhere along the way, I began to see that the various experiences and discoveries in those uncharted waters with my sister took me to a place that proved to be invaluable. The duties and responsibilities required for this divine assignment stretched me and made me grow in unexpected and indescribable ways. Consequently, this great change compelled me to share my story with others in hopes that they, too, would discover some of the secrets of the heart, come to appreciate the power of love, and, yes, even enjoy this difficult and rewarding journey.

This book is intended for caregivers. With some variations, I hope the reader will be able to relate to the situations and find encouragement in the prayers, scriptures, and suggestions. Since this is an account of my personal experiences providing care at home, it specifically speaks to those providing care for loved ones in that setting. Still, it is certainly beneficial for anyone who has a heart and concern for others needing care. It is for all who feel called to step in and do for others what they are no longer able to do for themselves—all who the Word beckons in Matthew 25: 37-40, which says: *"Then these righteous ones will reply, 'Lord, when did we ever see you hungry and feed you? Or thirsty and give you something to drink? Or a stranger and show you hospitality? Or naked and give you clothing? When did we ever see you sick or in prison and visit you?' And the King will say, 'I tell you the truth, when you did it for one of the least of these my brothers and sisters, you were doing it to me.'"*

As anyone might imagine, over seven years of providing

24-hour care to a person, a wide and varied range of emotions and situations will arise, providing ample opportunities to bring out the best and the worst in us. I chose to highlight some of the situations that I believe had the most impact on my life. While some situations helped me see the good in myself, others showed me that there was much room in my heart and soul to cultivate more kindness, gentleness, and self-control. In other words, it provided an opportunity for me to strengthen my love walk. Although I provided care for my mother until her passing, it was not until I took care of my older sister that I experienced what seemed like a spiritual awakening. It was caring for her over the span of seven years that I became much more aware and in tune with my spiritual growth and development. During this time, I also learned about the emotional, mental, and spiritual aspects of aging. Vicariously, through my sister's trials, I learned what it meant to love unconditionally.

When caregivers accept or find themselves appointed to this role, all of the attention defaults to the care recipient, sometimes with minimal or no preparation for the caregiver. The urgency or intensity of the situation may require immediate action, leaving the caregiver unaware and unprepared for the road ahead. This book is entitled ***Sisterly Love Endures, Guidance for the Caregiver*** because of the dedication, sacrifice, and unconditional love needed to care for others effectively.

Within each chapter, you will find a section entitled *"Guidance for the Caregiver,"* where I provide tools, suggestions, resources, and aides not only for you but for the person in your care. This section should help you to navigate through the caregiving process with more ease and confidence. It will enable you to embrace the importance of taking care of yourself so that you are then able to take care of others.

It is well known by most people that caring for oneself requires a delicate balance in all aspects of life. Well-rounded care includes spiritual, physical, social, emotional, mental, and financial elements. While I was challenged to maintain balance in all of the elements, the spiritual element seemed to be the foundation and driving force for all others. Whether you are considering caregiving or currently providing care to a family member or one with whom you have a kinship, you may find that prayer is critical to maintaining a balance in all elements that support the state of wellness. It is only then can you guide another along the path to healing. My experience taught me that sticking to the spiritual discipline of prayer and devotion early in the day, and sometimes throughout the day, strengthened my faith and provided encouragement and comfort during challenging times.

During your transition to becoming a caregiver, it is easy to lose yourself and your identity as you become absorbed in your patient's needs. As much as possible, I struggled to stay connected to friends, social events, and other resources that served to provide balance and emotional support when needed. When these connections were lost, I realized I was vulnerable to depression, loneliness, anger, isolation, and frustration.

Although I took pride in being strong, independent, and

slow to ask for help, caregiving showed me how to humble myself, put pride aside, and allow others to help me when needed. There were times when I was so knee-deep in the journey that I didn't realize how much I needed a break. Maintaining positive, loving relationships leaves the door open to ask for help during those times.

As challenging as this situation was, I experienced new joy as I learned more about myself, my sister, and, most importantly, the power, love, and sovereignty of The One who makes it all possible. Caregiving was an opportunity to be a blessing, be blessed, and ultimately an opportunity to develop a more intimate relationship with God. In this new relationship, God took me to a place in my soul where He could touch and change my heart. I understood and accepted that God's gift of love to us is undeniably one of the greatest of all gifts. What I did not understand was when love is alive in our hearts, like actors on a stage, we actively live out His word in 1 Corinthians 13:4-7 and all it says about love. I learned that love makes the situation better and bearable and helps us to see God in each other. Love never gives up and never fails. This lesson was more valuable than anything else I could have imagined.

One of my greatest challenges as a caregiver was trying to develop a trusting relationship with my sister. Lack of trust in any relationship can be crippling, especially when total dependency and vulnerability are at stake. Whether the care recipient is a relative, significant other, or stranger, the caregiver must show themselves as sincere and trustworthy. I believe this can happen when we are able to imagine ourselves in the other person's shoes. Unfortunately for me, this revelation came late in the process. In God's time, I learned to seek Him for wisdom in knowing how to gain my sister's trust. As my relationship with God blossomed, so did my sister's trust in me. My takeaway from that situation taught me that having a loving relationship with God will govern all other relationships. Only then could I manage difficult situations with care, honor, and respect.

Over the course of the relationship, I understood that my sister was frustrated, afraid, and angry, as she had to relinquish her control and independence to me. That combination of emotions had all the ingredients that made the job extremely hard for me as the caregiver and her as the patient. Sometimes, it seemed impossible to move past our disagreements, but with a sincere heart and fervent prayer, I discovered love really does conquer all. As my relationship with God grew deeper, I discovered that faith in His power and trust in His word enabled me to do what He was asking me to do. The Spirit reminded me of Hebrews 11:1, which says… *to have faith is to be sure of the things we hope for, to be certain of the things we cannot see.* Strong faith helped me to move forward despite the severity and gravity of whatever I was facing at the time. My faith continued to steady me even when decisions were difficult and resources were scarce. Toward the end of this journey, my mustard-seed-sized faith taught me that God could be trusted to meet each need, as He gave me abundant grace to do what He had called me to do, especially in the darkest hour.

Just as God provides spiritual gifts for us to build up

others and material wealth to share with the less fortunate, it was clear to me that this story was meant to be shared. So, it is with great anticipation that the caregiving experiences shared in this memoir will inspire others and help strengthen and encourage them as they journey through this difficult yet rewarding process.

How Do I Answer the Call? My Sister Needs Me

Spiritual Reflection

Do you have the gift of speaking? Then speak as though God himself were speaking through you. Do you have the gift of helping others? Do it with all the strength and energy that God supplies. Then everything you do will bring glory to God through Jesus Christ. All glory and power to him forever and ever! Amen.

1 Peter 4:11

Let me set the stage by telling you that I was born in New Orleans, Louisiana, the second of three siblings and better known as the middle child. I had an older sister and younger brother. After graduating from college, I left home and relocated to Maryland. In 1995, my mother had a stroke that left her unable to walk. Since I had been blessed with the best mom on Earth, I considered it an honor and great blessing to move her in with me. I took care of her until she passed in 1999. After my mom's death, I felt it was on me to make an effort to keep in touch with my siblings. Sister was twelve years older than me, so we were bonded as siblings but not very close. Besides the fact that we both had a strong commitment to family and enjoyed being girlie girls, we were almost as different as night and day. I was outgoing and enjoyed socializing and engaging with people. As we journeyed along together, God uncovered more shortcomings, negative emotions, and weaknesses about me that I never knew I had. I suppose my ego blinded me. Sister, on the other hand, enjoyed family gatherings but shied away from social groups. She was slow to get comfortable with people, but it was easy for her to love them when she did. She was quieter, introverted, moody, and a bit self-absorbed, but she was quite generous, which I always admired. She seemed to show love by giving money, so if she loved you, she showered you with unexpected treats from time to time. Both my brother and sister were much more giving than me. As time went on, I think Sister taught me generosity. Most of all, it was Sister's moodiness that was always a challenge for me because I never knew how to approach her.

Moodiness notwithstanding, Mama always instilled in us a sense of unity and caring for one another. Since I knew she would have wanted us to stick together, I visited Sister as often as I could. Somewhere along the way during visits, I began to see pronounced signs that Sister's health needs were changing. She had an abundance of prescription medications that she could not explain, and doctors' appointments were more frequent. I chalked this all up as normal wear and tear on the body, but it was clear that I would have to visit more often. The Spirit was preparing me to take a more active role in her life. I knew the day would come when Sister would need more care and attention. I began to wonder how we would get along with each other. As her health continued to decline, her tendency toward stubbornness increased, and she refused to follow the doctor's orders or do what was in her best interest or well-being. After surgery for knee replacements, she refused to follow through with physical therapy, so she eventually lost strength and mobility in her lower body. Three years later, it came as no surprise to me when she was declared physically disabled.

Since my younger sibling was unable to help at the time, the bold handwriting was on the wall, and it was aimed in my direction. I found myself entertaining the thought of stepping in to provide ongoing care for her. At the forefront of my thoughts was concern for how I would manage her moodiness and sometimes mean-spirited attitude. I put all of this on the back burner but kept a close eye on her as she went from having one knee replacement surgery after another, developed diabetes and incontinence of her bowel and bladder, and struggled with high blood pressure.

During one visit home, I noticed she was no longer able to use the walker or even walk at all. The writing on the wall was now a blinking neon sign. My saving grace at that point was that she had the support of a loving, devoted husband. Unfortunately, he was also not in the best of health and required ongoing medical attention, but he remained steadfast in his love and commitment to her. Several times, I offered to have her stay with me for a while to give him a break, but he refused. Needless to say, I continued to pray for them and hoped God would keep her husband strong. His role had changed from husband to caregiver. Since he also had serious health challenges, I began receiving nudges from the Holy Spirit that alerted me to prepare for change.

As life would have it, in early winter of that year, Sister's husband died of congenital heart failure, leaving her alone. One month preceding my brother-in-law's death, my marriage ended in a tumultuous divorce, and in June of that year, I retired from thirty-two years in education. As anyone could imagine, I was looking forward to some well-deserved rest while engaging in some of the activities retirees enjoy. Just as I felt myself coming up for air and beginning to look forward to a new chapter in my story, life took a turn for my sister, and with no further need for nudging from the Holy Spirit or writing on the walls, it was clear life had also taken a turn for me. Trips abroad, lunch with friends, and trusting God for a new mate had to be put on hold. There was no time for any of that.

Eleven hundred twenty-two miles away, my sister was living in an apartment alone, unable to walk, with no other relatives close by. She refused to pay for someone to sit with her. It was not a matter of what to do, but how should I get started and what should be the priorities? My saving grace in this situation was that I could see it coming and was mentally prepared—well, sort of. As I thought about the situation, I was reminded of something my mother used to say when faced with a problem. *"There is no use in crying over spilled milk; it will still be there when you finish crying."* Her wisdom taught me not to whine and complain but to roll up my sleeves and get busy. So, that's exactly what I did.

Since this book is more about my spiritual transformation during the time I cared for my sister, I will not go into a lot of detail about my time with my mother. Although, I should mention that both experiences were totally different. My mother had a very gracious and loving attitude with a healthy sense of humor. She was very appreciative of the least act of thoughtfulness and was never demanding.

Sister's attitude and temperament were quite different. In retrospect, I now understand why the time with my sister had such a powerful impact on my life. Her quiet, deep-thinking nature seemed to pull me closer to her to understand her way of thinking and challenged me to figure out what pleased her. She forced me out of my comfort zone. After all my years of teaching children and adults, I realized that caring for Sister would require that I learn new skills. Looking back, as difficult as it was to care for her, she helped me tremendously to be more open-minded about things that are different and to welcome adversity as an opportunity for growth.

Little did I know at the time, God had positioned me to grow by leaps and bounds. In providing care for my mother, I quickly discovered that it was more difficult than I expected. I was prepared to assist with the fundamentals of daily living, such as bathing, eating, and transporting her from home to various places. However, I was not prepared for the toll the situation would take on my emotional, social, mental, and spiritual health. Through good friends and great blessings, I was able to have affordable help with my mom while I went to work during the week. By the time my sister needed care, the situation was different. I was retired, which automatically made me the primary caregiver. With only one other sibling and no other available family, I realized early in the journey that I would need all the strength, endurance, and faith I could muster. As a believer, I learned early that prayer was essential in all situations and, most importantly, where life-changing decisions were concerned. My first action step was to pray for guidance, then seek advice from others about where to begin.

Lessons Learned

"Love is kind." Although I was called upon to take care of my sister when the time was inconvenient, the task seemed overwhelming and unpleasant, and my sister could be difficult. My love for God and her sustained me and helped me to respond with kindness. I also learned the power of obedience. When I prayed for wisdom and guidance, my flesh briefly considered placing Sister in a nursing home. As I heard the answer to my prayer, I knew a nursing facility would be an easy way of solving the problem of dealing with a sometimes-cantankerous sister. On the other hand, I knew in my spirit and soul that she deserved more personal care only I could give her. That *Still Small Voice* assured me it was the will of God, and He would see us through.

Meditation Moment

If you find yourself suddenly thrust into being the sole caregiver, consider reciting my prayer below, making it personal and relatable to your circumstances.

My Prayer

Most gracious and all-wise God, ______________ is in trouble and needs me. Father God, I know this comes as no surprise to You. You knew this day would come, and I know You've already worked it out. I need You now. Help me to know the plans You have for us—plans for a future and hope. Show me Your wisdom in making this important decision. My trust is in You and You alone. Let me not lean on my understanding. Take control of my thoughts so that my words and actions align with Your will for us. As You guide me through this process, Lord, help me be obedient to Your word that tells me to commit everything I do to You. Lift up ________________ at this difficult time in life. Give him/her comfort and peace. Let him/her feel Your refreshing presence in his/her life, loving him/her through this difficult time in a way that only You can. Let peace and harmony prevail in our hearts and home. Lord, I love You, trust You, honor You, and surrender this situation to You so that You may be glorified in it. It is in the name of Jesus and on His authority that I ask these blessings. AMEN.

Guidance for the Caregiver:

- ✓ Pray for guidance. Seek godly counsel through clergy or a trusted friend.

- ✓ If possible, arrange a family meeting to consider all options and develop a plan of action. The plan might include whether the care recipient will live in an assisted living facility, nursing home, or remain in his/her home with support. If possible, perhaps another family member could move in with the care recipient, or maybe the care recipient can move in with different family members on a set schedule.
- ✓ Consider what modifications may be needed in the home to accommodate the person's physical needs.
- ✓ Communicate with the primary care physician to ensure that medical appointments and all medications are up-to-date.
- ✓ The doctor may refer the family to a social worker or agency that will assist with the need for medical equipment, such as oxygen, hospital bed, walker, wheelchair, Hoyer Lift, etc.
- ✓ If not receiving Medical Assistance, call the Office of Social Services to determine eligibility.
- ✓ Determine if a power of attorney is needed to make decisions about finances and medical concerns.
- ✓ Call the Department of Aging to see what resources are available for support, i.e., respite care, transportation to medical appointments, and volunteer sitters.
- ✓ Subscribe to the National Alliance for Caregiving to network with other caregivers about services and creative ideas that will provide support for caregivers and care recipients.
- ✓ Contact local agencies that provide information and

support for the condition or problem you are dealing with, i.e., cancer, heart, aging, Alzheimer's, mental health issues, kidney disease, etc.

- ✓ Take Cardiopulmonary Resuscitation (CPR) training and become certified in CPR through National CPR Foundation.com. This can be done online for a nominal fee.

Additional Readings: Wisdom from the Word

I discovered that the word of God was my best resource as I faced this difficult decision. The following scriptures will provide emotional support, assurance that God is with you, and give you peace as you begin to take steps on your journey.

Psalm 16:7-8
Proverbs 3:5-7
2 Corinthians 9:8
Psalm 25:4-5
Philippians 4:6-7
James 1:5-6

Adjusting to a New Lifestyle

Spiritual Reflection

Call on me and I will answer you, telling you great and unsearchable things that you cannot know about, things to come.

Jeremiah 33:3

After some research about moving forward, my next major challenge was convincing my sister that she could not continue living alone in her condition. She could not understand that she was in great danger in not being able to defend herself against a potential intruder or escape to safety in case of a fire or another emergency. She received the services of a 4-hour home health aide and visiting nurse, but she needed 24-hour care. I purchased a Lifeline subscription for her; however, she did not understand that she needed to wear the device in order to have quick access to get help if needed. All of that added to a lack of trust in me and fear of the unknown, making the discussions long and draining for both of us.

After weeks of talking to her and praying to God, she finally consented to come to my residence but with reservation. While her decision gave me relief, I was a bit anxious and overwhelmed with having so much to do. It was now mid-summer in Maryland, and we decided she should come before the weather got cold. So, we targeted the move-in date for September. With no time to waste, I proceeded with the transition by closing out her apartment in Louisiana, including all bank accounts and services, packing and shipping clothing and necessary equipment, consulting with her medical team, and arranging flight transportation. No small feat, but with constant prayer for wisdom and guidance, patience and understanding with her reservations about the move, some adjustments to my schedule, and several trips back and forth, I managed to make it happen.

My home was a six-thousand-square-feet, two-story structure with very spacious rooms. Connecting each section of the home was a set of two to four steps. The master bedroom suite, which was my bedroom, was located on the first floor with a large bathroom and lots of closet space. However, the shower was in a sunken tub. This would be challenging for Sister because I had no way of getting her in and out of the tub. The second-floor bedroom was also spacious and had a walk-in shower, but the shower could not accommodate a wheelchair. I considered converting the side porch into a bedroom, but it required insulation, a full bath, and wheelchair access to the rest of the house. Regardless of what I decided to do, I needed more money than I had. I was at a crossroads, so you could probably guess what I did next. Yes, I prayed for wisdom and discussed my options with a few trusted friends. I decided the first-floor master bedroom suite would be more suitable and less costly to renovate. After doing some comparison shopping for an affordable contractor, the plan was set into motion.

But there was a more important question. Since I had not budgeted for any of this, how would it get paid? Taking some time to think and consider my options, the answer came to me through the wisdom of prayer. I could cash in funds from my retirement package. Problem solved. The answer to that prayer was, however, a mixed blessing. I was relieved to know funds were available but disappointed that I had to spend the money I planned to fund my dream trip to Italy. Admittedly, I felt a little guilty for feeling ungrateful. I asked the Lord for wisdom but wanted it on my terms. That would have to be resolved later. The greater blessing was that God was at work in my heart because there was a time when I would not have been able to part with that much money unless it served only my purpose. By the grace of God, I tightened my purse strings and continued to pray my way through.

Having no more time for guilt or disappointment, my faith kicked in, and I knew the trip to Italy would happen in God's time; He would make a way. Consequently, I regained focus, and the preparation for moving Sister began.

Since Sister was coming under duress and was a "girlie girl," I wanted to ensure that her room was as bright, cheerful, and as comfortable as possible. I purchased a new bed for her and enjoyed shopping for window treatments with coordinating bed linens in as much pink as I could find because that was her favorite color. While I shopped, the contractors built and installed ramps over the stairs inside and outside the doors. My move from the master suite to the second floor involved painting, purchasing an additional TV, and paying to have the bedroom furniture moved upstairs. While I put forth maximum effort to make Sister's new home warm and inviting, I also worked to create a comfortable new environment for myself, with earth tones and soft feminine accents.

According to schedule, by early September, Sister was finally moved in, and it was no longer just me and Zeus, my cat. Sister completed the family. Within one month, the honeymoon period was over. The difference in our personalities soon caused friction. We were almost like oil and water. As I mentioned previously, I'm more extroverted, and she was the introvert. Since there was no other family to serve as a buffer, I was pressed to find a way to make our relationship work. My constant prayer was for her to be happy, know how much I loved her, and that we would get along well together. In managing our differences, I learned to respect and honor her on days when she didn't feel like talking or moving, and she tolerated my need to talk and be in control—well, most of the time.

A more critical challenge for me during this transition was learning how to manage my time to ensure that her needs were met while taking care of the home and addressing my personal needs. During the first six months of her moving in, my schedule left very little time for sleep. Since my sister was incontinent, I got up several times during the night to make sure she was comfortable and dry. This unexpected challenge was an awakening for me. I found myself praying for grace to get adjusted to handling her bodily functions and dealing with accidents in bed when I did not get to her in time. That required some creative thinking about how to leave her dignity intact.

One night, to my surprise and dismay, she became irritated with the disruption of her sleep. I found her attitude very odd. Who would want to sleep in a wet bed? Well, I decided to let her have it her way. Since I wanted to keep the peace at all costs, I knew I had to find ways to keep her clean and dry through the night without waking her.

For the next several mornings, I was greeted by wet bed linens and an unpleasant smell in her room. Sister seemed to be alright with this, but it did not work for me. I kept a clean home and was always a fanatic about odors. This was just not acceptable. Through trial and error, I decided to limit her liquids after dinner and freshened her up at bedtime. This bedtime ritual included a sponge bath, adding extra bed pads under her, and supplementing her undergarments with a heavier nighttime sanitary pad. Putting myself in her place, I imagined this must have been uncomfortable for her, but she never complained. This strategy usually kept her dry until morning and surprisingly diminished the odor.

In order to get her up, bathed, and served breakfast by 9 a.m., I was up before 6 a.m. to have prayer, devotions, and exercise. This rigorous schedule caused me to experience burnout rather quickly, but the spiritual discipline helped sustain me. Planning and preparing meals, trips to the pharmacy, managing her doctors' appointments, food shopping, and keeping up with the laundry and extra linen changes consumed most of my days into the evenings. My caregiving duties left little time for my regular activities. I was beginning to feel resentful and guilty for not loving the process the way I thought I should.

If there was ever a time for prayer, this was it. I constantly prayed for grace. Of course, because God is loving, gracious, and merciful, He answered my prayer. Over time, as I read scripture and shared my trials and frustrations with trusted friends, I began to find peace. Friends prayed with me and offered to sit with my sister to give me a break. Though I was grateful for the break, the most profound answer to my prayer was a slow and steady transformation of my heart. It was softened, and my attitude changed. I found myself beginning to enjoy the process and taking pride in managing the various tasks that once used to bring me to tears. I was learning how to love. God did not change the situation; He changed me. This experience taught me a life-changing lesson that can best be summarized according to James 4:8: *Draw near to God and He will draw near to you.*

Lessons Learned

"Love always perseveres." Although the tasks seemed overwhelming at first, love lifted and enabled me. I could not give up.

Meditation Moment

My prayer below was focused on God's guidance according to His will. Say this prayer so God may order your steps with grace and clarity.

My Prayer

Merciful God, You are my shepherd, and I will follow You. I come now standing on Your promise, which says You will guide us along the best pathway for our lives, and You will advise and watch over us. I thank You, Lord, for encouraging me through Your promises, and I believe that they are true. Lord, I have answered Your call to take care of ______________, and I want to do it well. Give him/her the grace to follow my lead as I follow Yours. I believe by faith that You have prepared us for the road we must travel, and I thank You in advance for leading us beside still waters should we encounter any trouble along the way. Help me to provide care each day with love and tenderness. Order my steps and help me to organize my thoughts so that I complete each task well. Help me to remain calm and give me the patience to wait on You. Shower me with Your peace in the midst of my busy day and allow me to rest in Your care. I surrender this request to You and trust in Your word that tells me to *cast my cares on You because You care for me*. Lord, I pray that You will be glorified in all we do and even in the words we speak to each other. In the hope of my Lord and Savior Jesus Christ, I thank You, and I say Amen.

Guidance for the Caregiver:

- ✓ Take care of yourself first so that you are energized and have the right frame of mind to deal with the day's issues. Beginning the day with prayer, devotion, and exercise will give you a sense of wellbeing, peace, and strength. I like to say, "It makes me fit for service."
- ✓ Develop and try to stick to a schedule for managing tasks, incorporating time for breaks. Use a journal, day planner, or digital calendar to assist with providing structure. Having structure will help the day flow smoothly, along with getting tasks completed in a timely manner.
- ✓ If possible, arrange for someone to come in to give you time off, even if it's a couple of hours or a day, which allows you to run errands or just relax. Church members, family, and friends will be happy to assist.
- ✓ Consider adult daycare for one day of the week.
- ✓ Get help with chores.
- ✓ Plan meals ahead for the week. Try cooking several meals at once to avoid cooking every day. Look into meal prep delivery services.
- ✓ Coordinate nap time so the caregiver can rest or relax along with the care recipient.
- ✓ As much as possible, schedule appointments appropriately, allowing adequate time for daily routines without rushing.

Additional Readings: Wisdom from the Word

These scriptures will give you clarity in your purpose, help you stay focused on the work to be done, and increase your faith as you connect with God's will for this phase of your life.

Genesis 2:3
Psalm 90:17
Philippians 3:14
Psalm 32:8
Ephesians 1:10-11
Colossians 3:24

Caregiving with Grace

Spiritual Reflection

So, let us come boldly to the throne of our gracious God. There we will receive his mercy, and we will find grace to help us when we need it most.

Hebrews 4:16

I never had children, but my experiences as a special education teacher for thirteen years gave me a real sense of what it must be like to be a parent. At the onset of my journey with my sister, it occurred to me that caregiving was much like caring for a child. It required more than attending to basic living needs. I had to spend time with her. To foster a sense of family and try to strengthen our bond, I tried to do the things she enjoyed. This would have been a lot easier if I could bear watching the same cowboy movies every day or *Rocky* (which she could watch over and over). This bonding time usually put me to sleep within fifteen minutes of watching—definitely not much bonding going on. With more time for thought about this, I soon became more comfortable and creative with spending quality time with Sister. I capitalized on the girlie things we both enjoyed. Since we were both fans of rhythm and blues, I played music for us, especially during our in-house spa days. During our time together in "the salon," we reminisced about the music and engaged in conversation and laughter about the antics of the cat that we both loved. Those were times of great bonding. Sister had pretty feet and hands, courtesy of yours truly, and I liked making her feel good about herself.

Spending time with Sister was good, but I knew she needed more than what she was getting from the TV and me. She needed to be connected to the outside world. I was then faced with the challenge of providing opportunities for her to socialize with others. So, along with church services, we went to the movies, browsed at the mall, and I took her to social gatherings and events where she could meet other people. Soon, my friends became her friends, too. The greatest challenge came when Sister was not in the mood to go to social events, and there was no one to sit with her. On those occasions, I learned that sacrifice was a major part of caregiving. For all the events I missed, she still missed more. I had the ability to go where and when I wished, but she did not. This reality helped me to stay grounded in compassion and grace. Through it all, I tried to keep the focus on her needs while trusting God to care for mine.

At the same time, wisdom told me that time away from each other served a great purpose. It gave her an opportunity to make new friends as she interacted with the sitters and probably got a little more spoiled with the royal treatment she so much enjoyed. My friends affectionately referred to her as "The Queen," which would always put a big smile on her face. Meanwhile, I could decompress and enjoy a scene change. With this thought before me, I arranged time apart for us both to replenish ourselves whenever I could. Since we were both getting adjusted to our new lifestyle, this brief break in routine always seemed to come at the right time.

Lessons Learned

"Love always hopes." In the midst of trying to provide the best care that I possibly could, I hoped Sister would not feel like a burden or feel ignored. Instead, I wanted her to feel safe, secure, comforted, and, most of all, loved. I believe my prayers were answered. I learned in all circumstances to imagine myself in her place and respond in a way I would want others to respond to me.

Meditation Moment

When I think about the amazing grace of God, it beckons me closer to Him in prayer. Seek Him with your whole heart.

My Prayer

Heavenly Father, I come now in the name of Jesus, thanking You for Your amazing grace and mercies that are new every morning. I thank and praise You, Lord, for blessings seen and unseen. Lord, I want to understand how to meet ________________'s social and emotional needs. I believe I can do all things through Christ who strengthens me as long as I put my trust in You. Give me the grace to be sensitive to his/her thoughts and feelings. Anoint me afresh with creative ideas that will inspire joy, unity, and peace in our home and our hearts. Let the warmth of Your lovelight burn within us. Make us one with You. As we bond together in love, I pray You will be magnified in the things we do and say. I ask these blessings in the name of Jesus, and I say Amen.

Guidance for the Caregiver:

- ✓ Keep the lines of communication open so that there is understanding about the person's needs and desires.
- ✓ Look for fun things to do together, i.e., board games, puzzles, movies, arrange a visit with friends.
- ✓ Try not to put off spending quality time together. Consistently include it into your schedule each day or several hours each week.
- ✓ Surround yourself with like-minded people that will provide encouragement and support to you when needed. This will also help you to maintain a positive attitude.

Additional Readings: Wisdom from the Word

Providing care for the whole person requires thought and creativity. Let these scriptures guide you. Then allow your heart to follow accordingly.

Galatians 6:2
Colossians 3:23-24
1 John 4:12-13
Philippians 2:4
Hebrews 6:10-11
James 1:5

Caregiving with Love When She's Having a Bad Day

Spiritual Reflection

Give me understanding and I will obey your instructions; I will put them into practice with all my heart.

Psalm 119:34

Just when I thought I had gotten into the rhythm of caregiving and was managing to keep up with my life on the sidelines, every now and then, the journey would take an unexpected detour down a seemingly dark road. Sister would wake up in a bad mood, and there was no way to change direction. I believe the reality of the debilitating aging process pounced on her harder than usual sometimes. This made for hard days for us both. On those days, I fondly remembered something my mother used to say to us: "You got up on the wrong side of the bed today." In sharing that with Sister, the memory always made me smile, but it did not have the same effect on her. On those days, nothing seemed to go right from the time the sun came up until bedtime. She would ask for foods she couldn't have and complain that I didn't care about her. There were moments when tears would flow with no provocation or warning, and she was unable to explain how she felt or what brought on the overwhelming sadness. The meals were not to her liking. She refused her medication. She didn't want to bathe or change, and the list of complaints seemed endless. The saving grace was that the bad days were few. Yes, God knew how much I could bear. On those days, all I could do was offer words of comfort and sometimes allow her to indulge in a favorite sweet treat, offer to give her a manicure, or suggest a trip out of the house. I think she appreciated the effort, but once the sour mood set in, she couldn't seem to shake it off. On one of those days, when the emotional floodgates opened in the doctor's office, he prescribed a mild sedative for her. That became a part of her regular medication regimen, and it seemed to help, at least with the crying spells.

As I reflected on Sister's situation, I guess it was only by the grace of God that she did not fall into a deep depression. She left home at the age of seventeen and established independence; therefore, she was accustomed to taking care of herself alone for over fifteen years before getting married. Even in the marriage, her husband affectionately referred to her as the "boss lady." Now she was at the mercy of someone else for everything she needed and wanted.

Understandably, having to give up all independence and control to me must have darkened her days with feelings of fear, uncertainty, anger, sadness, and perhaps even depression. In addition to that, she was pressured into moving to a place where she had no connections while still mourning her husband's death. Life for her at that time was probably a big bitter pill to swallow. As I thought about my sister's predicament, my heart was heavy for her. Empathy for her drew me closer into her world and allowed me to imagine myself in her place. It demanded that I summon all the compassion I could to help her.

Negative emotions sometimes overshadowed My sincere desire to help my sister. Although I was consistent in prayer, there were times when my emotions got the best of me. Sister could be so difficult that my compassion would take a temporary nosedive. Occasionally, I could imagine how Moses must have felt. While he was on assignment by God to lead the people of Israel out of Egypt, they were demanding and disobedient, causing him to lose his temper. Sister's attitude could push me to the point of anger. I would then find myself imagining what it would be like to visit her in a nursing home. My emotions were further fueled by the ill advice of well-meaning friends who told me that I should not allow myself to be a victim of my Sister's selfish attitude. On two occasions, in my distress, I was so overwhelmed with emotion that I fell prey to Satan's scheme to try to rob us of our relationship, which was already fragile. I allowed him to tamper with my compassion and cloud my judgement, resulting in an argument with Sister where I said things that still make me sad when I think of them. Even though I had the ability to rise above the anger and frustration of the moment, before I could gather my wits or even pray, Satan pounced on me. All I can say now is thanks be to God for His grace. I am grateful that out of His great love for us, He would bring me back to Him. Consequently, I prayed out of remorse, repentance, and with thanksgiving.

Getting through the difficult days for me was life-changing. As I learned to take everything to God in prayer, I also developed a hunger for anything that provided encouragement. It just so happened that, while on this journey with Sister, I read *Embracing the Cross While Dying to Self-Life* by Frances Flanagan Jolley. This book made a great impact on my spiritual development. I was inspired to search my soul and came to understand that my attitude needed to change. I could easily point out the speck in my sister's eye but could not see the log in mine. As God allowed me to see myself, I was saddened and disappointed that I did not like what I saw. Out of the depths of my heart sprang a new prayer request: *God, take away any thoughts, attitudes, perceptions, and desires from me that do not align with You.* The Holy Spirit helped me to see that those things must die in me so that God could replace them with more of His character.

As this process was taking place in my heart (and continues to do so), little by little, love was also taking on new meaning. Learning to let go of old familiar attitudes and emotions is extremely hard to do, but I believe it's critical for the serious caregiver. This seems to be an ongoing struggle for me even now. My constant prayer is, *Lord, let there be less of me and more of You.*

This renewed spirit in me caused me to consider that my sister's bad attitude was most likely minor compared to everything else probably going on in her spirit and soul. In speaking with a friend's father, who is twenty-two years my senior, he shared with me that there are days when he feels trapped inside of gloomy thoughts of aging and physical discomfort. Though he has no serious medical issues, he stated that he feels alone and sometimes unwanted. As I reflected on his comments, I imagined that Sister must have felt the same way.

When the caregiver is able to put themselves in the care recipient's place, it's easier to manage the challenges of a bad day with love and mercy. However, if you will allow me to be completely transparent, some days are just not that simple in reality. Caregivers are mere mortals who also have feelings and may have an occasional bad day, too. They are also plagued by aches, pains, malfunctions in the home, problems in relationships, weariness -- the list goes on and on. Yet, caregivers must tread lightly on their bad days. They cannot afford to forget their role in the situation. A role that requires them to keep it all together while providing comfort and support with the love of God. If you have been called to be a caregiver, know that He has already equipped you to do this by the power of His Holy Spirit, but without warning, if not careful, it is easy to become distracted and lose focus. Consider this an opportunity for a closer walk with God.

Lessons Learned

"Love is not easily angered." My love for Sister helped me to forgive her for treating me badly. Despite the negative feelings and emotions I experienced, I could not stay angry and resentful toward her. Even today, when I don't receive the response or treatment I think is deserving, my love for people reminds me that they just might be having a bad day. I also learned to control my emotions. It's better for me to walk away or remain quiet when entertaining negative thoughts or feeling angry. I pray for the right words and time to address the situation.

Meditation Moment

You will experience days where things aren't going as planned. Cry out to God. Ask for what you feel you need, then enjoy His refreshing presence as it washes over you. Give it a try. Take time to go to a quiet place and pray. It works. It's also okay to call a friend you can trust to just listen to you and validate your feelings.

My Prayer

God, we are having a bad day today. With all that's going wrong, Lord, I thank You for the grace to see all that's right. In the midst of the emotional struggles of this day, I thank You for the grace to stand on Your word, which reminds me that endurance develops strength of character, and character strengthens our confident hope of salvation. Help me, Lord, not to give into the temptation of allowing a negative and self-serving spirit to take control. Open the eyes of my understanding and give me the wisdom to know how to turn this day around. Help me to find the compassion I need to comfort and soothe my ________________. Touch our hearts, redirect our thoughts, and give us Your peace that passes all understanding. Help us to experience You afresh and show us how to rest in Your love today, trusting that You are in charge. I thank You for hearing my prayer and pray that You, dear Lord, will be exalted in all that we experience this day. Now, let the words of my mouth and the meditation of my heart be acceptable in Your sight, Oh Lord, my rock and blessed redeemer. In Jesus' name, Amen.

Guidance for the Caregiver:

- ✓ Keep activities of the day as simple as possible; eliminate anything that may add stress, including home visits from nurses, therapists, etc.
- ✓ Create a more peaceful atmosphere with candles, soft music, and essential oils.
- ✓ Encourage the care recipient to talk about their feelings. Listen with an understanding ear without offering judgement or condemnation.
- ✓ Allow the person time alone to reflect or get an extra nap.
- ✓ Offer to have a spa day (pedicure, manicure, hair appointment, if possible.)
- ✓ Try to break the monotony. Get out of the house and go to the movies or lunch. Take a walk or go for a scenic drive.

- ✓ Order a special movie from TV with popcorn or a favorite snack.
- ✓ Arrange a telephone call or visit from a friend that may have a calming effect on the care recipient.
- ✓ If the number of bad days seem to increase, consult the doctor to assure there is no need for medical intervention.
- ✓ Pray and sing together.
- ✓ Imagine yourself in the other person's place. That should take you a long way.

Additional Readings: Wisdom from the Word

These scriptures will give you hope for change, peace in the moment, and strengthen your faith to endure. Just allow the Holy Spirit to comfort you as you read them. Find a few favorites and memorize them. They will come in handy when you are not able to read.

Psalm 23:4
Proverbs 18:10
1 Peter 5:7
Psalm 46:1-3
Nehemiah 8:10
Hebrews 12:1

Life Goes On

Spiritual Reflection

"Lord, help!" they cried in their trouble, and he saved them from their distress.

Psalm 107:13

We've all heard the expression 'And life goes on.' No matter how wealthy or poor we may be, what catastrophes may fall, or what status we may claim, life goes on. In other words, life does not stop to acknowledge challenges or wave a banner of celebration for victory. Whatever is destined to happen will happen, and we must keep moving forward. Giving up is not an option, no matter how overwhelming or impossible the challenge may seem. During the time I took care of my sister, as if life was not challenging enough, I discovered that everyday life issues seemed to magnify just when I felt like I could not handle one more thing. The flip side of this was that I discovered a reserve of strength and endurance I never knew I had. A wave of peace would blow over me that was beyond my understanding. I felt a strong resolve that enabled me to meet difficulty head-on with calm and sound judgment. I believe it was part of God's plan to push me out of the comfort and safety of my nest to show me that I was capable and ready to fly. Time and time again, He proved He had already equipped me for this journey.

In addition to meeting the challenges of finding my rhythm in providing around-the-clock care to my sister, life presented me with everyday problems, which all alone would have been enough to push me off the edge. In the midst of managing every detail of Sister's life, my regular life went on, occasionally without me—or at least that's the way it seemed at times.

As a homeowner, some things needed repairs due to normal wear and tear. I was nursing a roof problem, but I thought things were under control until one Sunday morning, I was awakened by loud crashing and crackling noises. I followed the noises up the steps to the top of the bridge on the second floor, and to my utter horror, I discovered the roof had literally collapsed. As the caregiver, I cannot tell you what a terrifying ordeal that was for me. Naturally, since Sister could not walk and I could not carry her, my immediate concern was getting her out of the house to safety. Even though she was on the first floor, I was not sure how stable the structure was and if it would come crashing down to the first floor. I began to call on the Lord for wisdom, and a blessing was already waiting. When I was able to calm down and think clearly, I called John, my then friend who later became my fiancé, who came right away. He assessed the situation and determined that he could temporarily jack up the roof. As he did this, he assured me that we were safe, and there was no need to move Sister.

After getting several roofing companies' estimates, I hired one that gave me an estimate of $30,000. (Did I mention I was retired?) Since my heart did not stop at the sound of those numbers, I found the strength to move forward. By God's grace and mercy, I was approved for a loan to have the work done. Until that point, I had given myself a *high-five* for planning carefully to retire in peace with no outstanding debt. Yet, only a few months after retirement, I found myself staring at a debt that would take an exceptionally long time to repay. The great blessing in that situation was that I was loan-worthy. Yes, God is faithful, and He always makes a way.

I survived that major catastrophe; however, life continued to remind me and prove to me that my faith would sustain us, no matter what happened. Later that year, during a winter freeze, the water lines froze. That posed no threat or major damage, but I had to call and pay a plumber. Then mysteriously, the electrical system went haywire, and some of the main outlets stopped working. During a brief windstorm, a huge oak tree fell across the driveway. Though there was no damage to the house, the roots pulled up a large portion of the driveway and smashed ornamental bushes that had to be replaced. Before I could recover from that, my beloved cat got sick. Thank God he bounced back, but not before needing medication and several trips to the vet. During the summer of that year, a storm caused a power outage that lasted for eight days.

With every incident, there was a question of how all of this affected Sister. I was agile and able to adapt, but it was no longer just myself. When Baltimore Gas and Electric (BGE) could not tell me how long the power would be out, I went into survival mode. Since our water came from a well, we also had no water when we had no power. Not having running water for one day was somewhat manageable, but it turned out to be more than one week, which was not sustainable. I considered going to a hotel, but when I thought of Sister's problem with incontinence, I decided I could manage better at home.

Through it all, I learned to remain steadfast. With fervent prayer, I rested in God's amazing grace and the blessed assurance from that *Still Small Voice* that He was in total control and would not fail. In fact, during the power outage, out of necessity, I discovered newfound resourcefulness. Giving no thought to whether chlorine would damage the septic system, I sifted water out of the swimming pool to flush toilets and set bottled water outside in the sun to warm up enough for Sister's bed baths. After a few days of this, I learned to get as much done as possible before nightfall. This resourcefulness provided opportunities for Sister and me to bond. We found humor in trying to wash up by flashlight. Surprisingly, she dealt with the major inconvenience very well. I am sure getting cool baths, eating fast food three times a day, and no TV was not exactly her idea of fun, but this was one of the few times she never complained. After each life event, it became clearer that God would keep His promise never to leave us or forsake us. I learned to lean on Him and follow his guidance. Even now, I am not easily rattled in the face of trouble. He taught me well. This too shall pass.

This great revelation does not mean I never experienced feelings of agitation, fear, and isolation. My faith increased over time. Making baby steps with trembling faith, I learned to take a deep breath and pray for guidance and help. Realizing that I was responsible for my sister's safety and welfare caused me to always think of her first. In times of crises, I noticed that if she understood what was happening and what I planned to do, she was cooperative and remained calm. Those life events also taught me to step aside, give pride a rest, and trust friends to help me.

My friend, Yolanda, whom I met at church and later worked with, used to always say to me, "Jessie, you are not alone." Although my faith was strong and I knew God was always with me, there were times when I felt isolated and emotionally vulnerable. I knew my friends were there when I needed to talk, but I did not want to be the kind of friend who always called with a problem or could only talk about my issues with Sister. I was also aware that each of them had their own problems, so sometimes, I was reluctant to call them.

When my days overwhelmed me with caregiving responsibilities, my world felt small behind closed doors, and all I could do was pray. What I did not understand was that God, in His infinite wisdom and omniscience, had placed people in my life who He knew I could call when the time was right. For instance, when the power was out in the summer, Yolanda and her husband, Joe, would bring us hot ice to keep the food cold in the refrigerator. God showed up in so many ways that I can't even begin to list them all. He knew beforehand that Marie, a friend of more than thirty years, would take care of Sister so I could take advantage of a temporary part-time job. Emily, another church member and bible study partner, would fall in love with Sister and sit with her so John and I could take advantage of an occasional evening out to the symphony. Yvonne, a former coworker and very dear friend, would arrange for her mother to sit with my mother while I went to work. Other friends called just to ask how things were going, and members and officers of the church called me to lift us in prayer.

Psalm 139 says that God examined my heart and knows everything about me—even my thoughts—before I speak, and He knows my needs before I ask. Consequently, out of His omnipotence, He predestined my journey with Sister. He knew other friends would offer to sit with Mama and Sister, and those who could not come offered to pay for sitters. Then there were "The Girls" who offered to pay for sitters so I could join them for birthday celebrations and time away when they could see I needed a break. Still, others sent money to meet whatever need we may have had. It took a while for me to see that I was never alone. I have such loving, loyal friends that I didn't need to ask for anything. I only needed to learn how to allow them to do what God had ordained them to do. Someone would always ask, "How can I help?" or give me an encouraging pat on the back by telling me that I was managing well. The moral of this story is that while life goes on, trust that God has a plan. Life's challenges come as a surprise to us but never to Him.

Lessons Learned

"Love always trusts." My love for God and His promises encouraged me that if I would just obey Him, He would see me through, and of course, He did, and I know He always will. I also learned that no one expects me to be strong all the time. It's okay to lay pride aside and allow friends to help me, and in return, it allows them to feel needed and valued as a trusted friend.

Meditation Moment

Caregiving can be challenging, especially when life seems to spiral out of control. God promises never to leave you nor forsake you. Commune with Him in prayer. Trust His promises.

My Prayer

My God, I come now, in the name of Jesus, trying not to complain or panic. You know that (tell what the problem is ____________________). Show me how to stand firm, fear not, remain calm, and trust in You. Give me clarity in my thinking about what to do. Show me who to turn to for help.

Prepare their hearts and minds for my call, that they will respond with love, wisdom, and understanding. God, I thank You for keeping us safe while we wait, and I thank You in advance for the provision to do what needs to be done. I am standing on Your word that tells me to be anxious for nothing, and I acknowledge that all power and authority come from You. I thank You, Lord, for working this situation out in a way that only You can. My trust is in You, and I will wait for Your instructions. I ask these blessings and count them all done in the holy and sanctified name of Jesus Christ, my deliverer. Amen.

Guidance for the Caregiver:

- ✓ Make sure the care recipient understands what's going on so he/she is prepared for any changes that may need to occur outside of the normal routines.
- ✓ If living alone, make sure someone you trust has a spare key to the home or apartment for emergencies.
- ✓ Prepare for emergencies with extra drinking water, a packed suitcase, a list of medicines, and important phone numbers handy in several places in the home.
- ✓ Pray and try to remain calm.
- ✓ Don't forget to apply CPR techniques if necessary.
- ✓ Keep the care recipient calm and assured that everything will be alright.
- ✓ Sometimes, the stress of what's going on will raise the stress level of the care recipient. Be familiar with the signs and symptoms when the care recipient is in distress or having a medical emergency, and don't hesitate to call an ambulance.

- ✓ If possible or necessary, call a friend to seek wisdom or physical support.
- ✓ Arrange time away to decompress and unwind as soon as possible after the crisis is over or under control.

Additional Readings: Wisdom from the Word

When feeling frightened or alone, these scriptures will remind you that God knows what you're going through, and He is there to help you. Find comfort, strength, and peace in your spirit as you read.

Psalm 34:8
Isaiah 40:28-31
Romans 8:28
Proverbs 17:17
John 15:13
Romans 8:31

Well-Meaning Help

Spiritual Reflection

Because of God's grace to me, I have laid the foundation like an expert builder. Now others are building on it. But whoever is building on this foundation must be very careful.

1 Corinthians 3:10

God gives you what you need. While on this caregiving journey, I experienced something about people that I found interesting and noteworthy. As the word got out about my journey with Sister, we captured the attention of onlookers and cheerleaders, family and friends, who meant well by offering unsolicited advice and criticism. I later realized that although they had our best interest at heart, they did not understand that problem solving was always easier from a distance. I knew they were caring, loving, and sincere people who meant no harm when they offered advice or criticized my way of doing things. Yet, they sometimes only annoyed me and fanned the flames of distrust in my relationship with Sister. As the caregiver, I was up to my neck in the situation and tried to stay positive. The last thing I needed was the added pressure of second-guessing myself or having to do damage control after someone suggested that my procedures were too harsh.

For instance, sometimes during family gatherings or visits, someone would feel compelled to criticize and tease me because they thought I was too strict with my sister's diet or that she needed to get out more. In keeping peace and controlling my emotions, I learned to remain calm and give a soft reply. As with many people with diabetes, Sister had a strong sweet tooth and enjoyed high carbohydrate snacks and drinks. Since she was obviously unable to manage her diet effectively, it was up to me to see that she maintained a healthy balance while enjoying some of the things she liked in moderation.

What some people did not know was that I was fighting a battle in my relationship with Sister. She was never really at peace with the reality that she could not live alone. Having her in the middle of the discussion about sweets only encouraged more emotional distance between us. So, when they teased me about being the food police, Sister felt I was not being kind to her by denying her the things she most enjoyed. I calmly explained to them that it was my job to monitor her blood sugar levels. In our early days together, Sister was considerably overweight. I had to remind them that lifting her from bed to chair and in and out of the car was not easy for me. Still, some people could not remember that or ignored me and would insist one more slice of cake could not hurt. Because they remembered how much she loved sweets, they also wanted her to know how much they loved her. On occasion, she would receive sweet treats as gifts, leaving me with the responsibility of limiting portions or explaining that she could not have it every day. Thanks to people I believe really cared for us, I was made to look like the mean one. It was difficult to help her understand that she was not being punished. I found myself explaining to her over and over that her medical condition would be compromised if she was not careful with her diet. She did not believe me, even when I reminded her that our mother also had diabetes and her leg was amputated because of a sore that never healed. Sometimes she seemed to understand, and other times, she was angry, all of which could have been avoided without the "help" of friends and family.

Since people could not see the daily challenges we faced, they did not understand why I did not take Sister out often. At one point, Sister was able to stand with support and swivel from the bed to the chair; however, over time, she gradually lost all strength in her lower body and could no longer assist me in transferring to the chair. To give her a change in scenery, I would take her to the kitchen for breakfast or to style her hair. This involved pushing the wheelchair up a steep ramp over three steps and a short distance to the next ramp over two more steps. Though it does not sound difficult, her body's weight required that I mustered all the strength I had to get up the ramps. Although I considered myself strong and physically fit, on three occasions, I slipped, and the chair began to roll backward toward me. To avoid the chair turning over, I fell to my knees to gain more leverage and control. Needless to say, on each occasion, my knees and back took the brunt of the fall, and I ended up in Urgent Care at least once.

Then I shall never forget the Sunday when we were dressed for church. While on our way to the car, the wheelchair turned over. That scary fifteen-minute ordeal seemed like an hour. Life was happening again, and we were in trouble. As hard as I tried, I did not have the strength to get her up. We lived in a community where the houses were spread far apart, so going to a neighbor's door for help was not practical. All my friends lived at least thirty minutes away. Calling any one of them was also out of the question.

I prayed a desperate prayer for help. In response to my plea were instructions from that *Still Small Voice* telling me clearly to get a footstool out of the bedroom, lift her from the ground to the footstool, and then up to the chair. (I am still amazed at how God works when we are in relationship with Him.) Feeling grateful that nothing was scraped or broken, I was then able to get Sister back inside, change her clothes, and proceed on to church. There was no doubt in my mind I had experienced an encounter with God that caused the roots of my faith to grow deeper and stronger. As scary and unsettling as that situation was, Sister remained calm. I think she knew I would find a way to help her.

Considering all we had been through, I understood that God gave her opportunities to trust that she was in good hands, while giving me opportunities to see that He was always with us and had everything under control. After a few more near misses, wisdom whispered to me to be careful about moving Sister around unless someone could be there to help me. Therefore, I decided to curtail moving her and kept transfers to a minimum. Without discussion, I believe Sister understood that trips out of the room and house would have to be well planned. Consequently, to keep my back and body healthy, I could no longer get her into the chair and up the ramps to other parts of the house as frequently as in the past. Not knowing this, family members would occasionally visit and comment that she needed to get out more. The former me would have served them with stern or sarcastic reply. Instead, I surprised myself when I let the criticism go unchallenged. At that point, I knew God was my vindicator, and no explanation was necessary as long as Sister and I were in accord. I decided the best course of action was to stay calm, continue to pray, and trust that God was giving me the ability to complete the assignment according to His plan.

From a different perspective, another group of friends constantly expressed sincere concern for me. They commented that I looked tired, and they could see signs of wear and tear in my countenance. Out of love and concern for both of us, they suggested I send my sister to daycare for a few days a week. It would provide opportunities for her to meet others and engage in social activities with people her age while giving me a much-needed break. I was encouraged by this suggestion and felt it was a good one. Sister, on the other hand, was not receptive to the idea, and I was not willing to force the issue. Keeping in mind that I was still working on earning her trust, I thought it was best to let it go. I never wanted her to feel that she was a burden or unwanted. Since this was such a great solution to a problem, my friends encouraged me to press harder on Sister. They believed she would like it if she gave it a try. The pressure was then on me to help them understand that if Sister didn't want to go, it was not worth the battle to convince her. In the end, I knew it would not give me peace to know she was unhappy. All things considered, I believed people felt helpless and just wanted to make the situation better in some way.

My great blessing in both of those scenarios was that God had supplied me with a garden of people who all served to remind me of His love for us. As the advice, suggestions, and comments continued, I learned to use discernment. I graciously thanked them for the information and continued as guided by the Spirit. I learned to take it all in stride, use what was helpful, and let go of the rest. The journey continued according to the Master's plan. All was well.

Lessons Learned

"Love is not proud." I learned that pride caused me to occasionally give an emotional response that was not related to the situation but was born out of resentment and anger.

Resentment that someone would have a bird's-eye view of the situation and feel justified in passing judgement or angry that someone would have suggestions without offering real help. I needed to feel that I had everything under control when in actuality, I didn't. Pride beckoned me to nurse resentment and carry the weight of the world on my shoulders. As I surrendered all to God, I was able to hear clearly that others may have been sent into my situation to open my eyes and heart to a fresh perspective. There was no prize in knowing everything. To my delight, I discovered that people offered advice in love. Some were there to remind me that I was not on that journey alone. I carry this lesson with me today. Godly love is not proud.

Meditation Moment

When receiving advice from friends and family, know that it is mostly coming from a good place. Take your discernment to the throne of grace.

My Prayer

Lord, I am committed to doing what You ask according to Your instructions, and I thank You that we are not alone because You allow others to support us and encourage us along the way. Bless them as they come. Send them with a sincere heart and loving spirit. I believe Your word that says your sheep know your voice, and no other will they follow. Help me to discern when You are speaking. Show me how to lean on Your word that says I must tune my ears to wisdom and concentrate on understanding. Strengthen my resolve to stand firm on Your instructions. Give me the grace to humble myself so that I can allow others to do what You have appointed them to do for me. Show me how to trust You more. I praise You for what You've done for us and thank You in advance for what You're going to do. Lord, you do all things well, and You are awesome in all of Your ways. My hope is in You. I pray that You will be magnified in all things concerning ______________________. In Jesus' name, Amen.

Guidance for the Caregiver:

- ✓ Before rejecting a suggestion, give it careful thought; try to receive all suggestions with grace and thanks. Some will be valuable. (*Remember that a gentle answer deflects anger, but harsh words make tempers flare. Proverbs 15:1*)
- ✓ Do not entertain negative comments or criticism. This only serves to disturb your peace and interrupt your focus.
- ✓ Learn to graciously avoid people that cause you to question yourself or bring you down.
- ✓ Remember that most people genuinely care for you and your loved one, and they mean well.
- ✓ Continue to pray for wisdom and guidance. Your heavenly Father will never steer you in the wrong direction.

Additional Readings: Wisdom from the Word

Spending quiet time in the Word of God will give you understanding and wisdom in making decisions for your loved one. Let His words help you to discover peace and discernment in your interactions with others when they express care and concern for you. Through these words, the love of God will help you to manage each situation with grace and forgiveness.

Psalm 111:10
Philippians 1:9-10
James 3:17
Proverbs 3:13
James 1:5

Caregiving with Courage When Health Begins to Decline

Spiritual Reflection

Woe to me because of my injury! My wounds are incurable! Yet I said to myself, this is my sickness, and I must endure it.

Jeremiah 10:19

I considered Sister's medical issues secondary to safety; therefore, my primary concern and reason for taking her in were that she was not safe living alone and unable to walk. Since the medications had stabilized her diabetes and high blood pressure, I knew she would be fine with regular follow-up visits to the doctor. When my primary care physician, whom I had known for over twenty years, agreed to accept her as a patient, I was thrilled and saw this as a God wink, especially because the doctor was no longer accepting new patients. How awesome was that? When God gives you an assignment, He will clear the way for you, leaving you with no excuses.

All she needed then was just some good TLC. By the time we hit the three-year mark, it seemed each passing week, month, and day brought on new changes. Sister's appetite remained the same, but she was losing weight. She developed annoying side effects from various medications, such as a continuous and annoying cough, sleeplessness, and headaches. To address these concerns, we made frequent visits to the doctor. In an effort to give her some comfort and relief, the doctor ordered more lab tests and adjusted her medications. For me, this created a time-consuming domino effect since trips to the pharmacy became more frequent and the regimen for medication more demanding. All of this brought on changes in routine and the need for more support and resources to maintain a reasonable standard of living for Sister.

In between being attentive to her medical appointments, I also had my share of doctor visits. I took Sister with me to my appointments in earlier days, and I trusted that she was okay alone when I left home to make a quick run to the pharmacy only ten minutes away. When Sister required more intensive care, I placed my doctor's appointments on hold, or in some instances, I hired someone to sit with her so I could keep my appointments. When her health became more fragile, I was not comfortable leaving her, even for a short trip to the store, so I managed to have the medications delivered. During the last two years of her life, Sister had several episodes of stroke-like symptoms. On each occasion,

I called 911, which led to a hospital stay for at least a week. With each hospitalization, the doctor felt it necessary to have a home nurse follow up with her or order physical therapy and speech therapy. Sister was never happy with the interruption in her normal routine of watching TV, so she was cranky and uncooperative with the therapists, but she would tolerate the nurse.

After careful thought about this situation, I realized it would not be effective for her because she had no interest in therapy. It would only be an unnecessary hassle for all involved, so I supported her decision to refuse service. Fortunately, the primary care doctor understood and pledged his support. This eliminated the embarrassment of her behavior and took me off the hook from making excuses for her lack of cooperation. Although it was to Sister's disadvantage, it gave her peace and saved me the challenge of persuading her to receive the extra support.

This entire chain of events took a toll on her and required extra time, attention, patience, and understanding from me. Since some medications had to be given every six hours, my sleep patterns were adjusted accordingly, and fatigue became my mainstay. There was no way to compromise the time. Though I was up throughout the night, our day started at the same time each morning. Consequently, I was sleepy most of the time. During the day, additional time was required to change bandages for pressure sores on her legs and schedule appointments with the nurse, specialists, and have bloodwork done. Caregiving now operated with more intensity. I started most days physically drained and ended the same. In dealing with my weariness, I wondered how Sister was mentally handling all of the changes. As time progressed, she was quieter and more withdrawn. I was no longer concerned as much for myself as I was for her. God was indeed softening my heart.

Six months later, Sister reached a point where she didn't want to put forth the effort to keep appointments. That became yet another struggle. It felt like a losing battle trying to help her understand that she needed help, and it was my responsibility to get her to the doctors so she could feel better. On several occasions, out of frustration, Sister commented that she knew she was dying. I had heard many times that people knew when the end was coming. Her comment gave me reason to pause. I was on alert but tried to assure her that she was alright. Here again, that familiar *Still Small Voice* suggested that I should pay close attention to her. Although she didn't wish to attend church regularly anymore, she had faith in God, and apparently, she had her own connections with that *Still Small Voice*. This realization gave way to a new awakening. I was convinced that Sister knew something that I didn't know. It was now time for me to trust her feelings.

Accompanied by this new awakening was more thoughtfulness about her needs and generally more compassion for her. After all, I was overwhelmed with the physical aspect of her care, but Sister was probably overwhelmed with emotion and maybe even afraid of what was happening to her. She insisted on keeping her feelings to herself, but I could often tell by her facial expressions when she was consumed by her thoughts. Occasionally, I could see that she had been crying. With each new medical condition, lab reports and specialists seemed to have no answers -- only medication adjustments and more tests. It was obvious by her periods of deep thinking and tear-stained face that this process was beginning to take her further away in her thoughts.

As the caregiver, I was also beginning to face reality. There was an unexplainable heaviness in my spirit that caused me to put things in perspective, especially while experiencing an overwhelming state of fatigue. However, I was still in a better situation than Sister because I was healthy. As the journey took us on more twists and turns, my love and compassion for Sister grew stronger. I began to search within myself to find the courage to help her move forward with as much comfort and peace as I could give.

One month later, we reached another roadblock. During a regular visit to the doctor to monitor her blood sugar levels and blood pressure, we learned Sister's leg was fractured. (It remains a mystery how and when it happened.) As a course of treatment, the doctor recommended that she wear a leg brace. Unfortunately, the leg brace created pressure on several places on her legs and caused pressure sores. This sequence of events brought us to an unexpected temporary stay in a nursing facility. Due to Sister's history of diabetes, the doctor felt intense wound care would help avoid any serious complications and expedite healing. Since insurance regulations would not approve the nursing home stay without additional treatment, physical therapy was prescribed.

Needless to say, Sister was very agitated and unpleasant. She managed to be cooperative with the staff but reserved her displeasure and irritability *for me*. Visits were difficult. She demanded to go home, refused to speak to me, and was argumentative. I must admit, Sister's surly attitude made it difficult for me to stand firm in my newfound compassion for her, but I loved her and had to forgive her attitude. I had to rise above my ego and understand her position. She felt like she was dying, and she wanted to be home where she was comfortable. She wanted to live on her terms. So, I had to allow Sister to be Sister. After seventy-seven years, she knew of no other way to be, and I had to accept that. By God's grace and mercy, we survived that ordeal and returned home with love and compassion intact.

Two months after she was discharged from the nursing home, her toes became so infected that I thought amputation was inevitable. Although the doctor never spoke that word, my concern was confirmed by the look on his face and the nurses' faces. My heart hurt for my sister. I could see she was in much pain. As I prayed for her, I was prompted by the Holy Spirit to speak life and healing over her as we bathed and changed dressings each day. Within weeks, I could see healing taking place in her toes. What a blessing that I did not give in to what the situation looked like to my natural eyes but instead summoned my faith and trusted in the prayers I said over her. It remains inexplicable to me that getting less sleep, dealing with more "bad days", and sacrificing more of what I wanted or thought I needed caused me to love more deeply.

Watching her health decline tugged at my heartstrings in ways I could not describe, but it certainly brought the situation into clear focus for me. Sister's body was breaking down, and love prevailed. It screamed for me to shift gears and show Sister in every way possible that she was not alone, that I cared for her, and would be with her until the end. Consequently, when weariness and doubt crept in, as it was certain to do, and bid me to complain, I rested on the peace and encouragement from the word of God. Sometimes that *Still Small Voice* would remind me that *"He who refreshes others will himself be refreshed," Proverbs 11:25.* Or one of my highlighted scriptures seemed to glow in neon lights as I read, *"Love never gives up, never loses faith, is always hopeful, and endures through every circumstance," 1 Corinthians 13:7 NIV.* I was fully aware then that this leg of the journey was not about my discomfort or inconvenience.

My sister's concerns and welfare were paramount to everything. I also found strength, encouragement, and peace in Philippians 2:13, which says, *"For God is working in you, giving you the desire and the power to do what pleases him."* As you, the reader, are likely to find yourself at this stage of life with your loved one, I say, take heart; you will be strengthened in His might.

Lessons Learned

"Love never gives up." In the natural, my sister's situation looked dire, but faith taught me to continue to expect God and His love to show up. As I prayed over her wounds, I could see healing taking place. This lesson sustains me today in difficult and seemingly impossible situations. My true love for the persons involved and love and trust in God assured me that everything would be all right. I also learned that in the face of trial, I am selfless; I can put my needs aside for the needs of others.

Meditation Moment

There will come a time when the person in your care will visibly start to deteriorate, but God knows all. Go to Him in prayer, and He will give you peace.

My Prayer

Dear God, ____________________'s health is beginning to fail, but You already know that. Lord, I am weary, overwhelmed, and unsure of the direction we are going now. Your word says that You will never leave us nor forsake us. Let us experience the power of Your presence now, assuring us that You are with us every step of the way. Give him/her peace in his/her spirit and comfort in his/her body. Give the doctors, nurses, and medical staff the grace and wisdom they need to provide treatment with compassion, honor, and tender care. Help us both to endure the trials of this situation one day at a time. Your word encourages me to let all that I am wait quietly before You, for my hope is in You. Thank You, Lord, for giving me a steadfast spirit, strength, and peace during this time of great trial. You are Lord of all things, and all power and authority belong to You. I offer You this prayer in the precious name of Jesus Christ, the lover of my soul. Amen.

Guidance for the Caregiver:

- ✓ As previously recommended, call the Department of Aging to see what resources are available for support, i.e., respite care, transportation to medical appointments, volunteer sitters.
- ✓ Consult the primary care physician about a visiting nurse to assist with wound care or possible equipment that may provide more support, i.e., wheelchair, Hoyer lift, shower chair, oxygen, etc.
- ✓ Arrange time away from the patient, weekly if possible, to replenish your reserves that will keep you calm, relaxed, and refreshed.
- ✓ Install a baby monitor in the patient's room, which can be used to notify you of emergencies.
- ✓ Document any significant changes or patterns in vital signs (blood pressure, blood sugar levels, temperature) to share with the visiting nurse or doctor.
- ✓ Remember to update the list of medications as they change and keep the list in several places in the home.
- ✓ As the situation becomes more intense, it is important to stay connected to the outside world. Keep a trusted friend close for emotional and spiritual support.

Additional Readings: Wisdom from the Word

Now perhaps more than any other time, you will need encouragement, patience, more faith, and strength to endure. These promises will help you feel a stronger connection with God as you lean on Him and trust His grace and mercy to see you through.

Romans 5:3-4
2 Thessalonians 3:5
James 1:2-3
1 Thessalonians 5:18
Hebrews 10:36
James 5:11

Caring for Others When the Caregiver Needs Care

Spiritual Reflection

Don't be afraid, for I am with you. Don't be discouraged, for I am your God. I will strengthen you and help you. I will hold you up with my victorious right hand.

Isaiah 41:10

I was born into a family plagued with high blood pressure, arthritis, heart disease, and diabetes. Consequently, I knew at an early age that I had to take good care of my body, with hopes that I could escape some of these ailments, if not all of them. The bonus was that my past experiences in providing care for my mom taught me to be diligent in exercising self-care, or my body, mind, soul, and spirit would suffer. Armed with this knowledge caused me to make a serious commitment to maintain a healthy lifestyle.

Therefore, nurturing myself early in the morning was mandatory before I started my day with Sister.

I discovered that no amount of nurturing made a difference when the aging process seemed to move faster than real time. There was no way of escape. While in the throes of caring for my sister, I endured arthritis, gastrointestinal issues, migraine headaches, cataracts, and mysterious pains that were frequent unwelcome visitors, with insomnia always being the first one at the door.

As long as God was generous with His grace, I attempted to address each of them with a good attitude. Though the ailments were bothersome, everything seemed to be under control until the night an excruciating pain in my shoulder awakened me. I had never experienced this pain before and could not recall any injury or trauma that may have been the cause. Under normal circumstances, I would have gone to the nearest emergency room, but immediately, I thought about Sister. My pain would not allow me to get her dressed and into the car. I did not know how long the ER visit might be. I thought it was too late to call someone to stay with her. How could I take care of myself when she needed me to take care of her?

Despite my extreme discomfort, what I really wanted was to take care of my sister without the distraction. I continued to ask for comfort and wisdom while trying to think of what to do. I cried, prayed, and rested in God's mercy until the next morning when I could come up with a workable plan. By then, that *Still Small Voice* instructed me to get Sister up early, explain the situation to her, give her a bath and breakfast, then head over to Patient First, which was only five minutes away. I prayed for favor all the way. My prayer was answered when the doctor saw me quickly, gave me a shot for the unexplained pain, and sent me on my way with muscle relaxers, which he said would make me sleep. I was grateful for the relief, but I was concerned about how I would take the medication and be on alert to care for Sister. As God would have it, that extreme level of pain did not return for a long time. Tylenol kept things under control. When I needed something extra, I decided to take half of the muscle relaxer. It made me drowsy, but I was still able to function.

After that episode, my consistent prayer was that God would keep my body healthy and strong and my mind clear so I could remain fit for my divine assignment. Although I was and remain sure that God answers prayers and wants only the best for us, I continued to experience various ailments, such as broken toes, sprained muscles, intense itching, knee and back injuries, bee stings, and bouts of contact with poison ivy. Notwithstanding all of that, as God would have it, my heart was with Sister.

Just as this new resolve to put Sister first was taking up residence in my heart, my flesh protested. I found myself in a fight with conflicting emotions. I was resentful that I did not have the luxury of taking care of my needs, and I cried out to God, asking for forgiveness for feeling this way. At the same time, I asked for healing so I could continue to take care of her. I was an emotional wreck, but in hindsight, I know that is when God does His best work in the heart, mind, and soul. I had come to a place where my sister's needs were more important to me than my own, and I was still on a new trajectory of learning. My prayers were being answered that I die to self. With a slow and steady pace, I started understanding the meaning and relationship of unconditional love and personal sacrifice. God was removing some of the old me and replacing it with more of Him.

That revelation was good for my soul. Just like the metamorphosis of a butterfly from the pupa stage to adult, I was being transformed. This process took me to a deeper level in my morning devotions, prayers, and time spent with God. At every turn, I was beginning to recognize God's love, mercy, and grace for us. No, I don't mean He miraculously healed me or prevented me from experiencing any further discomforts or accidents. Instead, He allowed these experiences so that I could experience the fullness of His power in my weakness. It was during those times that I learned the power of surrender. Over time, I learned not to panic or allow stress to take control but rather to seek Him first and allow Him to guide me along the path to peace, comfort, and mercy. He had given me an assignment that included numerous opportunities to grow, draw closer to him, and stretch my spiritual muscles, all while taking care of my sister. How awesome is He!

As a result of those refreshing times in His presence, I was able to think clearly, operate with wisdom, and, as my mother would always say, "live to tell the story." Through each leg of my journey, I learned that God was my closest companion, and I learned to commune with Him constantly about everything. I learned that I could not fully appreciate and understand how merciful, loving, and faithful God is until the trials come. What a blessing to be able to "tell the story," and I hope you, the reader, will share your story, too. That's how we strengthen and encourage one another.

As I prayed for my sister's health, I had the blessed assurance that I was also in God's care. I could accept that I would need medical attention while caring for Sister, but my constant hope was that nothing would ever prevent me from giving her the care she needed. My love for her had caused me to become accustomed to her demanding ways. Somewhere along the way, I learned the meaning of unconditional and sacrificial love. Despite how difficult she could be, I spoiled her and lavished on her all the loving care I could give, and I could not imagine anyone else being able to love her as much as I did.

Lessons Learned

"Love is not self-seeking." I loved my sister so much that when I experienced a personal health challenge of any kind, my prayer was that God would heal me so I could take care of her. I learned that my caregiving experience was not all about me but a lesson in humility, compassion, and the power of sacrifice for others. In addition, God showed me how to trust Him in my time of need -- that when I am in my weakest hour, He is strong within me.

Meditation Moment

When feeling sick or medical issues occur, as they will, remember that God is a healer. Just as you trust him to heal your loved one, know that He will heal and comfort you, too. Go to Him in prayer.

My Prayer

Most merciful and loving God, I lift my eyes to You where there is help. I am calling on the name of Jesus, believing that there is power and healing in His name. In the name of Jesus, I am asking for healing in my ________________________. I know You have healed others, Lord, and because You love us all the same, I believe You want to heal me, too. While I wait for the manifestation of this healing, I thank You, Lord, for giving me comfort in my body, peace in my heart, and helping me to put my trust in You. I thank and praise You for loving me, saving me, cleansing me, and making my body fit for Your service. Your word tells me that my faith has made me well, and I know Your word will not return to You void but will go where You send it and do what You say it will do. I thank You, Lord, for Your love, grace, mercy, and hope, and I pray that in my healing, You will be exalted. In the name of Jesus Christ, my savior and my strength, I say Amen.

Guidance for the Caregiver:

- ✓ Get a yearly physical and follow the doctor's advice and recommendations to address any problems you may have.

- ✓ Call a friend or arrange a paid sitter, if possible, to sit with the care recipient while you go to appointments or just rest if needed.
- ✓ Consider taking multivitamins, herbal supplements, and teas to keep up your strength. Herbal teas are also good for relaxing and staying calm.
- ✓ Look for free workout videos on YouTube. There is something for every level of ability and interest.
- ✓ Join social media groups for added support.
- ✓ Plan an overnight stay at a nearby hotel or retreat center once a month.
- ✓ Host a get-together with family and friends once a month. Movie night with pizza, potluck, and game nights with snacks are easy to plan and require little to no preparation.
- ✓ Develop an emergency plan in case you are unable to provide care for any amount of time.

Additional Readings: Wisdom from the Word

God's words are packed with promises of healing and strength. Rest in His promises and find peace for your weary soul.

Psalm 30:2
Psalm 92:2
Malachi 4:2
Psalm 61:7
Isaiah 41:10
James 4:7-8

Caregiving When You Feel Overwhelmed and Worn Out

Spiritual Reflection

Then Jesus said, "Come to me all of you who are weary and carry heavy burdens, I will give you rest. Take my yoke upon you, let me teach you because I am humble and gentle at heart, and you will find rest for your souls. For my yoke is easy to bear, and the burden I give you is light."

Matthew 11:28-30

I thought I had earned her trust and that we had moved past certain friction that initially occurred between us. I failed to consider that during the great transition of me becoming her caregiver, I was the only one doing the intensive personal development work needed to be the best caregiver and be the best sister, friend, confidante, provider, and prayer warrior possible. But this extensive work was one-sided. Sister was still the same person she was when she arrived.

During certain situations, I would be caught off guard thinking that Sister understood our new normal. She would become agitated that she could not do what she wanted to do, and sometimes, her request would be irrational, such as draining her bank account due to a lack of trust with my financial management. I will admit that I was appalled and hurt when she did not want to cooperate without a struggle. I certainly anticipated that by then, my sister would have seen that my motives for taking care of her were purely based on love.

I loved my sister dearly, and I was happy to take care of her, but I could not understand nor appreciate her negative attitude. She caused me to question myself and wonder what I was doing that made her suspicious of my motives. My emotional response to this behavior surfaced in the form of resentment, which brought me to a place of discord with myself. Spirit and soul were no longer in agreement. Almost immediately, that *Still Small Voice* reminded me that I needed an attitude adjustment. Sister was allowed to feel what she felt. She owed me nothing, and the change of heart was on me. I was the fortunate one for having health, strength, and provision to care for her. Why then did I feel reprimanded by my conscience and Sister did not?

Well, thank God for friends. Out of my frustration, I called Yvonne, a long-time and dear friend who was also a caregiver for her mother. From time to time, we exchanged stories about our caregiving experiences, laughed together, and encouraged each other. I shared my feelings with her, and she told me just what I needed to hear. She told me that Sister's attitude was probably not about me at all, but she was perhaps distressed that she had relinquished all control. She was trying to hold on as long as she could, even if her judgment was cloudy. Looking back, I can appreciate that this situation was difficult for her.

I was able to admit that grace and forgiveness were in order. After my talk with Yvonne, the anger and resentment seemed to dissipate. Someone had let all the air out of my balloon, and I was disappointed in myself for being inconsiderate.

My spirit was in turmoil. How could I read scripture, pray every day, talk about the Lord's goodness to others, and then make this situation about me? Sometimes I needed a human touch after talking with God, but this time, I believe God wanted me to hear from the human first.

Through constant prayer for grace and strength, I made continuous efforts to understand Sister's perspective. However, as time went on, Sister's attitude became more difficult to bear. It seemed the harder I tried to go along with her, the harder she worked to make life difficult. She gradually progressed to refusing food after making special requests. It made me sad to see her so unhappy. Soon, I realized I was also unhappy, and I was failing at caregiving. I found myself gripped with fear and sadness that without change, our relationship would end badly.

Trouble was brewing, and I needed help. Praying was on autopilot at that point. I talked to God as though He was physically with me. In response to my prayer for guidance and godly counsel, I concluded that perhaps it was time to consider an alternative placement. Maybe this would be the right solution for all concerned. I was emotionally spent when one day, following a heated and ugly argument about her refusal to take her medication, I began to seek placement for Sister in a nursing home. I took a tour of the facility, spoke with the director, and asked all the necessary questions. The facility was new, clean, and close to home, but still, something was missing that I could not pinpoint. For several days, I pondered over this decision and sequestered myself to think and pray. I would usually consult a trusted friend, but not this time. Since God had given me this assignment, I needed to be 100% sure that He approved of my plan. Only the Holy Spirit could help me sort out my true feelings and guide me through this.

Suddenly, one morning, I was awakened by what seemed like clanging cymbals. Like reveille, God spoke to me in a voice that didn't seem small at all. I clearly understood that I had allowed selfishness to take up residence in my heart. I was frustrated that my sister would threaten my ability to be in control while she was exercising the only power she had left. She was tired of living and had decided that refusal of medication was a quick and easy way out. She was no longer able or willing to buy into the truth that God would call her home in His time, not hers.

Wow, that was hard to hear, but the truth is hard sometimes. My heart had opened wider, and love was becoming a permanent resident. Once more, through tears,

I repented to God for being hard-hearted and prayed for clarity, direction, and peace. Needless to say, not another word was spoken about an alternative placement. Sister remained home where she belonged. For a time, I dealt with guilt and shame for even considering removing her from my home, where she was loved and accepted. From that day on, I vowed to love and honor her to the best of my ability until death.

Lessons Learned

"Love is not rude. Love is not easily angered." When I was weary to the bone, God helped me remain steadfast in doing what needed to be done without grumbling, complaining, or being rude. Today, I am trying to remember to practice what I learned. It's sometimes better to suffer in silence than to allow weariness and frustration to spiral out of control and cause me to give in to behavior unbecoming of one who professes to be a follower of Christ. I realized that in the midst of darkness, the love light still glows warm and bright.

Meditation Moment

Over time, caregiving can be overwhelming. Fatigue and frustration can get the best of you. Go to God and tell Him how you feel. Ask for what you think you need. Then listen for His answer and rest assured that He hears you and cares.

My Prayer

Dear God, I love ____________________ and I know he/she needs me. Lord, everyone needs and deserves a place where they can feel wanted, loved, and secure, and I thank You that my home is that place for __________________. I need Your help. I am worn out from the day-to-day responsibilities of care that seem to become more demanding each day. I know You do all things with intention. Show me how to delight myself in You, in my work, and in my attitude. Let me not grow weary in doing well. Help me to show love and honor without grumbling or complaining. Touch my heart and renew the right spirit within me. Show me how to steal away with You when I am overwhelmed by the demands of the day. Let me not lose compassion for the situation but be more loving. Even when I can't sense Your presence or understand Your plans, help me to remain patient in confident hope that You are with us at all times. Let me not be distracted by anything or anyone that's not of You. I thank and praise You, Lord, and I ask these blessings in the matchless name of Jesus Christ, my comforter, strength, and peace. Amen.

Guidance for the Caregiver:

- ✓ Arrange time away from the house. Take advantage of respite care provided by the Department of Aging in your area.
- ✓ If possible, arrange daycare for the care recipient.
- ✓ Schedule time for regular, daily self-care (exercising, walking, reading, napping, etc.)

- ✓ Seek godly counsel from your minister or a trusted friend.
- ✓ Identify a prayer partner with whom you can pray at least once per week.
- ✓ Caregiving is not easy, and no matter how hard you try, it may not be for you. If you determine it is not a good fit, let love carry you through until you are able to make alternative arrangements.
- ✓ As a last resort, consider placement in a reputable nursing home. It's critical that you do extensive research first.
- ✓ If a nursing home is the solution, schedule frequent visits, and ask friends to visit as often as possible.

Additional Readings: Wisdom from the Word

God understands and cares when weakness overtakes us. Read about the grace, mercy, and strength He offers in our time of need.

Psalm 46:1-3
Acts 20:24
Hebrews 4:16
John 1:16
1 Corinthians 10:13
James 1:2-3

Caregiving with Trust in The One Who Provides

Spiritual Reflection

Let us not become weary in doing good, for at the proper time we will reap a harvest if we do not give up.

Galatians 6:9

As the journey continued, so did life's little surprises. When Sister's medical needs changed, requiring bandages for pressure wounds and even eye exams, I discovered that Medicaid nor Medicare would cover such expenses. Since Sister was responsible for maintaining her life insurance policy, occasionally assisting with sitters, sharing the cost of private transportation to church, purchasing toiletries, and managing other personal needs, her funds were limited. Therefore, the responsibility of all other expenses rested with me, including her copays for doctor visits.

When we started this journey, Sister and I agreed to share the sitter's cost when needed. We were blessed with loving and caring friends who volunteered to sit with her, and since I seldom went out for long periods, we only needed to pay sitters occasionally. Also, when I was no longer able to transport her in my car without help, Sister and I agreed to share the cost of private transportation to church.

Somewhere along the way, Sister, who was known for being the generous one, changed her mind and refused to stick to the agreement. This left me with the choice of staying home, which I did many times, or I could dig into my piggy bank and pay. You have probably figured out by now that caregiving can be hard on the mind, body, and spirit, and have unexpected financial implications. Getting a break out of the house for a while can be worth the investment.

It wasn't long before I decided that keeping peace and harmony in the home was more important than struggling with Sister about money. Love said she wins. Consequently, I used sitters less and learned how to entertain myself at home with movies, walks around the neighborhood, or in the company of friends when they visited me. Nevertheless, with increased utility bills, a mortgage, incidentals, and routine maintenance of the car and home (remember when the roof collapsed?), my budget started to scream for help. To this day, my soul looks back and wonders how I made it through, but then again, there is no need to wonder. I know it was the grace and provision of the Lord. Through constant prayer and great faith, God brought me through and continues to do so. Wisdom showed me how to find peace in the simple things, like playing word games, working jigsaw puzzles on my iPad, and reading Christian literature and suspense novels. The real icing on the cake came when I learned to enjoy the art of doing absolutely nothing for a while. That was challenging at first, but it had a great payoff when I got into the swing of things. All of this helped me get through hard days and gave us opportunities to know and love each other better. The favor and love of God were surely with us.

Spiritually, I was in a new place, and James 4:8 seemed to be embedded in my spirit: *Draw near to God, and He will draw near to you.* With His grace, God eased me into my divine assignment, and I could clearly see His hand at work on our behalf at every turn. These experiences served to enlighten me and helped me to see that the difficult journey of providing care did as much for me as it did for Mom and Sister. While they received the care and unconditional love they needed, I received a spiritual awakening -- something more valuable to me than money. It was inexplicable to me that I learned about the true love, great faith, and the magnificent power of the almighty God during the most challenging times in my life. In those difficult times, I learned how to trust Him, and I learned the power of prayer.

Lessons Learned

"Love always trusts." When my finances were stretched, I learned to continue to give generously in faith. Consequently, God showed me that He would provide. He did, He does, and I know He will continue. Like repeating a grade in school, that was a lesson I had to learn more than once for it to take hold. I am delighted to say I learned it well.

Meditation Moment

Anytime is a great time for prayer, but especially when you feel like your resources are depleted. Jehovah Jireh, the provider, will always make a way. Talk to Him. Then watch what He will do.

My Prayer

"Oh Lord, You are my God; I will praise You and exalt You, for in perfect faithfulness You have done marvelous things, things planned long ago." (Isaiah 25:1) Out of my distress, you showered me with grace, mercy, and love. So now, Lord, I come not asking for anything but to thank and praise You. My heart is overwhelmed with Your goodness, and for this, I give You glory and honor. You are awesome in all of Your ways. I thank You for being my provider, for keeping us safe, shining a light in dark times, and most of all, for filling us with Your precious Holy Spirit. You do all things well, and You never fail. Lord, I love You and thank You for loving us, too. May Your great name forever be praised.

Guidance for the Caregiver:

- ✓ Don't neglect to tithe and share with others in need. No matter how little you may have, you still have more than someone else. You will be surprised at how the financial blessings will flow for you.

- ✓ Check with The Caregivers Program in your area to see what resources are available.
- ✓ Network with church members and friends to identify needed resources, such as contractors, volunteers, and sitters.
- ✓ Periodically review expenses to monitor spending habits and assure that you are spending wisely.
- ✓ Pray and trust God to meet your needs.

Additional Readings: Wisdom from the Word

God has provided instruction, encouragement, and blessings in His word for every area of our life. See what he says about giving, being a good steward over what you have, and trusting Him to provide for you.

Deuteronomy 8:18
Matthew 6:31-33
2 Corinthians 9:8
Proverbs 19:17
Malachi 3:10
Philippians 4:11-13

Caregiving Until the End

Spiritual Reflection

For that is what God is like. For this God is our God forever and ever. He will guide us until we die.

Psalm 48:14

When all is said and done, we know that everything has an expected end. As the journey with Sister continued, doctors' visits and 9-1-1 emergencies became more frequent. Sister's body seemed to be on a downward spiral as she weakened and became more fragile. Healing then seemed inconceivable. Just as it is prone to do, the doctors believed that diabetes prevented the pressure sores from healing. In addition, Sister's blood pressure would spike to alarming readings, or her blood sugar level would rise above 200 for no apparent reason, when the normal level for her was a range from 120-140. Joining the list of ailments was a strong headache that was resistant to relief or comfort from any medication. Since I had also suffered from debilitating migraine headaches in the past, I understood her pain. On days when she complained of a headache, I frantically tried everything within my power to keep her comfortable, including making repeated calls to the doctor's office. I was distressed when nothing seemed to work. My love for her would rather accept her death than watch her suffer with no relief. No one deserved that, and she looked so miserable.

In mid-Spring of 2018, during a visit to the doctor, Sister was admitted to the hospital for chest pains. As I waited for test results, I received a visit from another doctor that caught me by surprise. Though he approached me with a warm smile and easy manner, his identification tag spoke to me before he introduced himself as the Palliative Care doctor. My antenna went up, and I could not take my eyes off his name tag. My limited knowledge about the medical field alerted me, and I knew at that moment that the current journey was taking us on a different route. In his best bedside manner, the doctor explained that Sister's headaches were caused by bleeding on her brain. Due to her fragile condition and age (78), surgery was not a viable option. In fact, it could cause more harm, and he could not guarantee that the bleeding would stop. Within an hour, I was speaking with a representative from a hospice care facility. The journey was picking up speed with no time to adjust emotionally or mentally. It's amazing how quickly the world seemed to turn upside down.

While trying to steady myself from this swirling motion in my head, just as at the beginning of our journey, there was writing on the wall. It prompted me to think about our age difference, which suggested Sister would most likely proceed me in death, but I rarely gave it any thought and certainly was not prepared for this. Despite this gloomy prognosis, I received the news with an unexplainable calmness, as if I had been waiting for the news. In the back of my mind, I wondered why I was not upset, moved to tears, or shaken at my core. I didn't have the courage to tell Sister about the prognosis, and she never questioned the change in routines when the nurse visited twice a week. Earlier in the journey, I was too busy to notice, but it became clear that God had prepared me all along.

If you recall, there was a time when Sister told me that she was dying and refused medications and treatment. I think God was preparing her, too. This leg of the journey had brought us to the point where the pressure sores would heal in one place and break out in another. Following the nurse's order for treatment of the sores was especially challenging because Sister did not like being turned every two hours and would not keep the pillow under her back, which was designed to hold her in position. Eventually, the sores on her heels cleared up, but the sore on her tailbone never did. In Sister's defense, it was almost impossible to heal that one because it could not receive adequate air and circulation that provided oxygen to the blood. All of that, in addition to the unexplained weight loss, I think were signs that her body was breaking down and death was imminent.

With a heavy heart, my immediate concern was that my sister should be as comfortable as possible. My constant prayer was that she would not suffer. As God willed it so, Sister was released from the hospital to come home with hospice services in place. Approximately one month after returning home, Sister began to transition. Standing by while my sister transitioned was a sweet time of loving her to the very end. Friends and family came over to pray for her and encouraged me to remain strong. The hospice nurse assured me that although Sister was in a coma-like state, she could still hear me. With this in mind, I spent time in her room just talking to her, singing, and praying. Even at this stage of the journey, it was my delight to be with her while she could hear me and be reminded of the sisterly bond we shared. This process lasted for a month or so before she answered the final call to go to her eternal home.

Certainly, this phase of life is different for everyone. If I had just a word of advice, I would say provide the most loving and responsible care all along so you will have no regrets when the journey comes to an end. Unfortunately, I do have some regrets. As I look back, I wish I could have been more tender and understanding at times when Sister seemed angry and frustrated. Sister could be a tough cookie, unbending, demanding, and unwilling to yield to the things that were best for her. I used to tell her that she was her own enemy. As I found myself preparing to continue the journey without her, I lamented over a few of the arguments when she was unreasonable and I was determined to be in charge. In the end, it didn't make a difference. Too bad it took me until she was lying on her deathbed to understand what she was trying to say. While I was healthy and strong, she was weak and powerless. Though I believed I was doing what was in her best interest at the time, I believe now that she probably felt small and without hope.

Regrettably, I was slow to understand that I needed to allow her to make as many decisions as possible so she would not feel such a sudden loss of independence and control. Through it all, my experience as a caregiver was rewarding and enriching -- an opportunity for me to have just a closer walk with Jesus and certainly worth doing all over again if He calls me.

All thanks and praise to God! He was and continues to be the best caregiver of all. The lessons I learned will serve me well. No matter what my future holds, I hope God will be glorified and magnified in the things I say and do as I practice what I learned on my divine assignment. While He guided me through caring for Sister, He took care of my soul.

Lessons Learned

Looking back on how Sister's life came to a quiet and peaceful end, I'm reminded of the beautiful and heart-stirring words of the Peace Prayer of St Francis of Assisi. The last line says, "...and it is in dying that we are born to eternal life." I believe my sister received eternal life. My lesson in her dying was about having another chance to live a more fulfilling, self-sacrificing life of service. With God's grace and power, I get a chance to move forward in a newness of life that shall serve the world better than I did before the journey began. My hope is that when my time comes to die, I will be spiritually and emotionally prepared, and my time on Earth will have reflected the lessons learned during this journey of love.

Meditation Moment

Here is a prayer for when the patient is close to the end of their earthly journey. Try to embrace this special time as you find solace with the Father.

My Prayer

Holy Comforter, my savior and God, we are coming to the end of this journey where we must part, and ____________________ will go home with You. I thank You, Lord, for the time we shared. Thank You most of all for walking with us through this journey. The challenges I faced and lessons I learned have blessed me beyond measure, and I would like to think that ____________________ was blessed, too. During this journey, I learned to see You more clearly and love You and others more dearly. As ________________ waits for Your call, Lord, please take away any fears he/she may have and replace them with Your peace. Let him/her smell the sweet aroma of your presence in the room. When the time comes, and he/she hears her name, I pray the angels will usher him/her gently away with singing and welcome him/her home with hugs, smiles, and a big fanfare. I can imagine he/she will be so excited to see ________________ again. Lord, I love You and thank You for loving us and showing us how to truly love each other. Most of all, I thank and praise You for the precious memories that will comfort me when she is gone. May the name of Jesus forever be praised. Amen.

Guidance for the Caregiver:

- ✓ If you have not done so, make arrangements for end-of-life services or celebrations (funeral, cremation, or donating the body). Make sure to consult with the patient.
- ✓ Make appointments with clergy, funeral homes to discuss plans.
- ✓ Notify family and friends that may wish to visit.
- ✓ If the person is alert and able to communicate, discuss what's happening with him or her, and allow them to make any final decisions they wish to make.
- ✓ Though you may have feelings of anger, fear, or regret, allow friends and family to comfort you.
- ✓ Take care of yourself. Get up early to spend time doing the things that give you peace and enjoyment.
- ✓ Spend time with God, allowing Him to lavish on you and give you strength and wisdom for the many decisions you will need to make.
- ✓ Lavish your loved one by spending time in his or her room, telling them what's on your heart, praying for them.
- ✓ Let love have its way; go wherever your heart leads you.
- ✓ Make sure you have a DNR on file, if appropriate.

- ✓ Keep all life insurance or other policies handy.
- ✓ If there is a last will and testament, ensure it is easily accessible.

Additional Readings: Wisdom from the Word

If you have not experienced death on a personal level, spend time reading these scriptures. They will give you the comfort, understanding, and peace you will need to help you through this difficult time.

Isaiah 57:1-2
John 11:25-26
1 Corinthians 15:54
2 Thessalonians 3:16
Revelation 14:13
Luke 2:29
1 Corinthians 15:42-44
1 Thessalonians 4:13-14
Romans 14:8

Epilogue

Reflecting and Looking Forward to the Future

Spiritual Reflection

Clearly, you are a letter from Christ showing the result of our ministry among you. This "letter" is written not with pen and ink, but with the Spirit of the living God. It is carved not on tablets of stone, but on human hearts.

2 Corinthians 3:2

As of this writing, in the Fall of 2020, I will soon be approaching the two-year mark of Sister's death. I still carry fond memories of our times together. I shall cherish memories of warm and tender times of worshipping together on special days; turbulent times of misunderstanding and anger that never lasted long; happy times of teasing each other and playing with Zeus, the family cat; and scary times of wondering if her wounds would heal or how I would get her out of the house as the ceiling was collapsing. There were loving times when I felt like I was getting it right, like when she was filled with delight while eating and enjoying cookies, ice cream, her favorite hard candy, or something new to wear. During those times, all was right with the world for her, and I learned that was really all that mattered. All things considered, I am grateful for the chance to stretch and grow. It bears repeating, I would gladly do it all over again. My sincere hope is that Sister went home knowing that I loved and cared for her with my whole heart.

At the time of Sister's memorial service, I was given good advice that I should not rush into anything but instead take time to mourn, heal, and gain strength for the next leg of my journey. As anyone would, I will always miss Sister. Writing this has been difficult at times, but I believe it is part of my healing process. I'm still not sure what lies ahead, but I look forward to traveling and writing more. My heart has been forever touched and changed by my caregiving experience. I would welcome an opportunity to work or volunteer with hospice, and I give all thanks and honor to God for shaping me and making me pliable in His hands. I want to be a part of wherever there is a need for healing, comfort, true love, and a heart for service.

As I consider the lessons learned along the way and think about where I am now on the trajectory of my life course, 2 Corinthians 3:2 (written at the top of this section) comes to mind. Going forward with whatever I'm called to do, I believe I am prepared for greater service -- for servant leadership. I pray for strength and pledge to show myself as a true letter from Christ -- not written with pen and ink on tablets or stone, but written on the hearts of men. What better way can we love God, ourselves, and others? I pray this book has been an inspiration of encouragement to you, and I hope you learn to fall more deeply in love with THE ONE who makes it all happen. I hope you enjoy the journey.

Acknowledgments

This book would not have been possible without the loyalty, love, and support of the special people God placed in my path along the way.

To my husband, John, for his unwavering support of my efforts to see this through. His incredible knowledge and skill with computers saved me the agony of lost files and navigating from one program to another. His obvious love for me inspired me in a way that leaves me speechless. My prayer partners, Yvonne Terry-Lewis and Sonya M. Armstrong, for keeping me lifted and encouraged in prayer three times per week.

Author and writing coach Jackie "JC" Gardner for her encouragement and sage advice to tell my story my way, and the generous gift of her time, wisdom, and contagious enthusiasm that helped me to believe in myself and to stay motivated until the end.

To Pastor Samson Doolin and my Faith Christian Fellowship World Outreach (FCF) Church family for spiritual growth, genuine warmth, and sincere love. They provided a place of grounding and encouragement for me in amazing ways.

Above all, I acknowledge and give honor and praise to God, my Father and creator, without whom I could do nothing, but with Him and through His Spirit, I can do all things, for He strengthens me.

Additional Resources

Alzheimer's Association: Provides free training and workshops that teach practical skills. **(Alz.org)**

American Association of Retired Persons: Provides free help for individuals taking care of a loved one. **(aarp.org)** For help with picking up groceries and receiving calls from a Friendly Voice volunteer, visit **aarpcommunityconnections.org.**

Department of Aging: Contact this organization in your local area for information and support services for seniors and people with disabilities (legal services, nutritional education, family caregiver support, transportation, community outreach programs, home delivered meals, and trainings).

Alison: Free online courses in various areas of caregiving, also course in caregiving certification. **(Alison.com)**

Care.com: Find local senior support.

About the Author

Jessie S. Myrick is a native of New Orleans, Louisiana, and currently resides in Pikesville, Maryland. She is the middle sibling of sister, Willie Mae, and younger brother, Harry. She is a retired educator and holds an M.Ed. Degree in Special Education and Administration and Supervision. As ministry leader of Small Group Bible Study and member of the Cancer Care Ministry, she is dedicated to service in her church. Jessie believes she learned to love and appreciate caring for others by watching her mother, who was devoted to caring for everyone she met. She provided loving care to her mother and sister until their deaths and continues to enjoy visiting friends in nursing homes and assisting with meals, laundry, and daily living activities for homebound friends or those recuperating from illness. Jessie enjoys traveling with her husband, John, keeping company with her beloved cat, Zeus, reading Christian literature, writing, and spending time with family and friends. This is Jessie's first book, and she believes there will be others to follow. If this book blessed you in any way, please reach out via email: *jessiewrites51@yahoo.com.*

CPSIA information can be obtained
at www.ICGtesting.com
Printed in the USA
JSHW050508240421
13842JS00003B/9